Introduction to Sewing

igloobooks

igloobooks

Published in 2015
by Igloo Books Ltd
Cottage Farm
Sywell
NN6 0BJ
www.igloobooks.com

Cover images © Thinkstock / Getty

LEO002 0715
2 4 6 8 10 9 7 5 3 1
ISBN 978-1-78440-283-9

Printed and manufactured in China

Introduction
to
Sewing

Contents

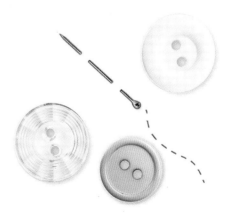

Introduction

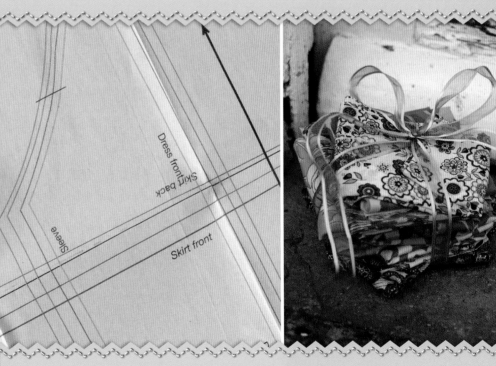

Dress front

Skirt back

Sleeve

Skirt front

Follow the step-by-step sewing instructions
in this comprehensive how-to guide and
learn to create your own stylish garments.

Needles

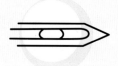

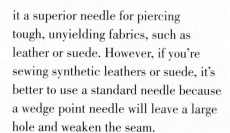

A ll you ever wanted to know about sewing machine needles but were afraid to ask!

A common mistake often made by beginners is to use the same needle for everything you sew. The size of the needle that you need for a specific job depends on the size of the fabric yarns in the fabric you are sewing. For example, if you are sewing a fine fabric then you need to use a fine needle, which needs to be fine enough not to mark the fabric and yet still have a big enough eye to ensure that the thread does not break or fray while you are sewing with it.

With so many different needles out there, all with seemingly bewildering names, how do you know which one to choose?

Sharp points (regular)

For use with woven fabrics because they cause a minimum amount of puckering and produce an even stitch without damaging the fabric. It is not recommended for use with knits because it can cause skipped stitches.

Sharp points are more slender through the shaft and should be used when edge stitching on woven fabrics, sewing on finely woven fabrics or heirloom stitching

very fine fabrics. They are also a good choice when sewing with synthetic suede. These needles come in varying sizes from the finest size 9 to the heaviest size 18.

Ball-point needles

Specifically designed to be used with knitted and stretchy fabrics. Ball-point needles have a rounded point rather than a sharp one so they push between the fabric yarns rather than piercing them the way the sharp points do. This eliminates any potential damage to knitted fabrics.

These needles should be used when sewing with interlock knits, coarse knits and other fabrics that will run if snagged. The needles come in varying sizes from 9 to 16. The larger the size of the needle, the more rounded the needle point is.

Wedge-point needles

Designed for use with leather and vinyl, these needles will easily pierce these fabrics and create a hole that will close back up on itself. The wedge shape makes

it a superior needle for piercing tough, unyielding fabrics, such as leather or suede. However, if you're sewing synthetic leathers or suede, it's better to use a standard needle because a wedge point needle will leave a large hole and weaken the seam.

These needles come in varying sizes from 11 to 18. The smaller sizes are suitable for softer, more pliable leather, while the larger sizes are designed for sewing heavy leathers, or multiple layers.

Embroidery needles

These have a larger eye to accommodate the thicker embroidery threads. They also have a special scarf (the groove above the eye) that protects decorative threads from breaking.

The size of the needle that you need for a specific job depends on the size of the fabric yarns in the fabric you are sewing."

Quilting needles

Also called Betweens, these have a tapered point that allows you to stitch through more layers of fabric (usually the quilt sandwich) and across intersecting seams. The tapered point prevents damage to pricey, heirloom-quality fabrics. They are usually smaller and stronger than regular needles, with a small eye, and come in sizes 9 (largest) to 12.

Universal-Point needles

Have a slightly rounded point, similar to the ball-point needle, and are used for general, everyday sewing of woven or knitted fabrics. The needle is tapered so it slips through the fabric weave of the knit easily while still retaining enough sharpness to pierce the cloth. They come in many different sizes with 14/90 and 11/75 being the most popular.

Size of Needle

Once you know which is the right type of needle to use for a sewing project, it's also important to know which size of needle to use. Although there are exceptions, as a general rule, the needle size is judged by the type of fabric being sewn.

MEDIUM-WEIGHT FABRICS

If sewing with slightly heavier weight fabrics such as gingham, poplin, linen, muslin, chambray, wool crepe, flannel, knits, jersey, wool, wool suiting or stretch fabrics, a size 14 needle is generally best.

LIGHTWEIGHT FABRICS

When using lighter weight fabrics such as synthetic sheers, batiste, taffeta or velvet, a size 11 needle would be the normal choice.

MEDIUM-HEAVY FABRICS

Sewing with fabrics such as gabardine, heavy suiting or tweed would require a size 16 needle.

HEAVY FABRICS

When using heavy-weight fabrics such as denim, ticking, upholstery or canvas, a size 18 needle is the most suitable.

DELICATE FABRICS

When sewing with extremely delicate fabrics such as silk, chiffon, voile, fine lace or organza, a fine size 9 needle would usually be the best choice.

Main image:
Invest in a variety of needles that are easy to keep organised – many packs also offer advice on which needle is best for which fabric.

Always replace a dull or damaged needle straight away. Damaged needles can cause skipped stitches and tearing of your fabric."

Fabric Types

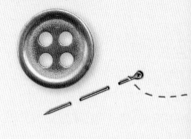

Do you know your burlap from your chintz, or moleskin from ticking? Here's our brief guide to the most common fabrics.

Brocade

A dense weave with the appearance of all-over embroidery. The silk version is most often used for formal wear, while you'll find the cotton version for upholstery.

Burlap/Hessian

Often woven from hemp, jute or raw cotton, it's best used for curtains, wall hangings and sacks. It's also a great base for embroidery.

Calico

A light cotton fabric used for children's clothes and home furnishings.

Candlewick

Famous for bedspreads, this tufted fabric is thick and soft.

Canvas

A heavy fabric that's most often made from cotton, but is sometimes made of a blend of natural and synthetic materials.

Cheesecloth

A lovely lightweight, loosely woven cotton fabric. Used for summer-weight tops and dresses, although as the name suggests, it was originally used in the production of cheese.

Chiffon

Made from silk or polyester, this formal wear fabric is light with a good drape. It works well for multi-layered garments, and for those with tucks and gathers. Use a fine needle to construct the seams.

Chintz

This most often floral-printed fabric is used for heavyweight curtains and upholstery. Synonymous with the English country cottage look.

Cotton

Comes from the seed pod of the cotton plant. It forms the basis for a plethora of fabrics, on its own in muslins and canvas, or spun with polyester.

Corduroy

A fabric with a rib effect, usually cut with the stripes falling vertically. Available in different weights – the heavier the weight, the wider the ribs.

Crêpe

Woven with a twist in the fibres, this fabric has an almost creased look to it. Sometimes it is backed with satin.

Crêpe de Chine

Mostly made from synthetic fibres rather than the traditional silk, this lightweight, plain-weave fabric is used for evening wear and blouses.

Damask

A firm weave of cotton, linen or blends, often forming a pattern with metallic or reflective areas. Often used for interiors, particularly table linen and bedding.

Denim

Famously strong fabric originally used for work clothes, now worn by everyone, whether for work or pleasure. Made with coloured warp and white weft. Use a denim-specific needle with a heavy cotton thread.

Drill

Similar to denim, this strong weave is made from cotton. There is usually a strong bias (diagonal) in the weave.

Felt

A wool fabric made by agitation and rubbing of the wet fibres; the application of heat fixes it. A great fabric for children learning to sew.

Flannel

Soft, pliable fabric made from wool or cotton blends. Always pre-wash flannel before working with it because it can shrink, but it can also stretch when worn. It's a good idea to add a little to the seam allowance because it has a tendency to fray.

Gabardine

A heavyweight woven twill that's the main fabric for raincoats and sportswear.

Gingham

Cute cotton fabric, woven to give an almost chequerboard effect. Used for cottage-style interiors and children's clothes.

"Always pre-wash flannel before working with it because it can shrink, but it can also stretch when worn."

Jacquard

Named after its inventor, Joseph Jacquard, this heavy fabric is woven on looms, with a raised surface and often with images. You'll find this fabric adorning upholstery in many stately homes.

Jersey

A common name given to 'knitted' versatile fabrics. Has a tendency to stretch width wise. It's best to hem jersey with a twin needle to top stitch.

Lamé

This name is given to fabrics that are woven with metallic fibres.

Linen

The fibres of the stalks of the flax plant are used to make this fabric. It's known for creasing heavily but it's possible to purchase some linens that have been blended with synthetic fibres that crease less. For best results, sew using a cotton thread with 9–12 stitches per inch.

Moleskin

No moles are killed in the making of this heavy fabric. It's actually cotton based, which is brushed to create a suede-like quality.

Muslin

A cotton weave that comes in various qualities. Dressmakers like to use it to make 'dummy' garments before cutting the actual, intended material to size.

Net

Most often made from nylon, this open, knotted fabric has hexagonal-shaped holes.

Polyester

A product of the petro-chemical industry, this fibre can take on the appearance of silk, blend with other fibres, or be turned into batting for quilts and stuffing for toys.

Satin

Not exactly a fabric type, but the name given to a particular weave of silk, cotton and polyester. Needle and pin marks will show on satin, so check all measurements before sewing. It's also a good idea to change your needle regularly to avoid it snagging.

Shot Silk

This is the effect achieved when the weft and the warp of the weave are different colours. As the fabric moves, it appears to change colour.

Silk

Comes from unwinding the cocoon of the silk worm. It's a strong yet delicate fibre, and has been discovered as being used over 5,000 years ago in China.

Taffeta

Made from cotton, polyester or silk, this fabric has a subtle sheen and rustles when it moves.

Ticking

The most common use for this fabric is pillowcases. It's recognisable by its white/cream background with blue stripes.

Tweed

Woven from pure wool, often with slubs of another shade running though it. Its hard-wearing nature makes it the perfect fabric for making suits.

Velvet

A weave with a short-cut fibre, traditionally made from silk fibre, but nowadays also woven from synthetics.

CHOOSING

Thread

There are many different types of sewing thread that should all be used for different projects. Join us in investigating some of the most commonly used ones.

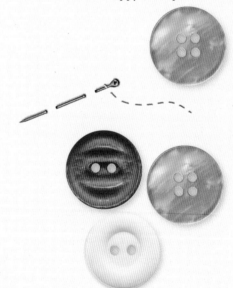

The type of thread that you use when sewing a particular project will be chosen based on the type of fabric you are using, and the project that you are sewing.

There are many different types of thread available to buy, but we are going to look at ones that you are most likely to use with your sewing machine. Thread comes in different thicknesses; general purpose threads tend to be medium thickness of about size 50. Cotton is the most commonly used thread and is available in a huge array of colours. You are most likely to use cotton thread if you are sewing linen, rayon or medium weight cottons.

Most cotton threads are mercerized, which means that the thread is smooth and shiny. It is not advisable to use cotton thread for sewing on jersey projects, as the jersey fabric is very stretchy and cotton has no stretch.

Fine silk threads are most often used for sewing on silk and wool. The make up of this thread gives it quite elastic qualities, meaning that it can be used on jersey fabrics with some success. Silk threads are also idea for basting stitches because it is very fine and so will not leave holes when you remove the stitches at the end of the project.

Alternatives

You also have the choice of using nylon or polyester threads when sewing light to medium-weight fabrics. Polyester is good for using on stretch fabrics, as well as knitted and woven fabrics. Many polyester sewing threads will be coated with silicone to minimize friction as you are sewing with them, allowing them to freely flow through your machine. Another alternative to cotton/polyester threads is a hybrid of the two. Cotton wrapped polyester gives you the best of both types of thread. It is strong and elastic with a tough, heat-resistant surface.

Cotton, polyester and the cotton wrapped polyester in heavier weights also available and are most suitable for sewing upholstery fabrics or heavier weights of clothing. If you are unsure which thread is best for your fabric, your local haberdasher will be happy to help.

"The type of thread you use in your next sewing project will depend upon the type of fabric that you are going to be sewing."

Basic Stitches

There are lots of different stitches that you can use to create a range of effects in your sewing projects.
The ones on these pages are some of the most popular.

Chain Stitch If you want to create thick, pretty lines quickly, this is the stitch to use.

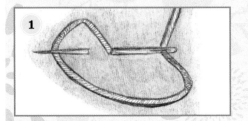

Step 1

Pull the needle to the right side where you want your chain-stitch line to start. Insert the needle close to where you brought it up and without pulling it through, bring the needle up approx 0.5cm (¼in) along the line, looping the thread under the point. Pull the needle through and tease the stitch to make it even.

Step 2

Now push the needle back through the fabric, very close to where it came up in the loop, and bring it up 0.5cm (¼in) along the line you are following. Loop the thread under the point of the needle again and pull the needle through, again teasing the stitch to even it out.

Step 3

Repeat step two until you have a length of chain stitches. Keep the stitches even by leaving the same 0.5cm (¼in) gap and teasing out each stitch as you go. Don't pull too hard on the thread as the fabric may pucker. To finish, secure the last loop with a little stitch at the top of the curve.

Split Stitch Perfect for making curved lines, flower stems and outline stitches.

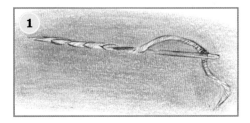

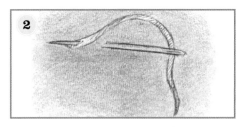

"Be careful when pressing embroidery with an iron, you could flatten the stitches."

Step 1

It's best to work from left to right. Start by bringing the needle through to the right side, at the point where your line begins. Take the needle down a stitch to the right, then bring it up halfway along the previous stitch, splitting the thread.

Step 2

Place the next stitch to the right of the first, taking the needle back up through previous stitch as before. Continue in this manner until your line is finished.

Satin Stitch Use rows of close, straight stitches to fill many different shapes for interesting embroideries.

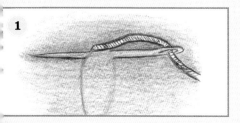

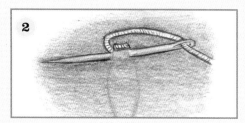

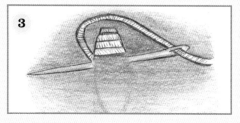

Step 1

If you are unsure about working freehand, use a fading marker pen to mark out your design. Starting at one side, at the top of your shape, bring the thread through to the right side and back down on the opposite edge of your design. Bring the needle up next to where you first brought the thread through.

Step 2

Insert the needle back through to the wrong side, close to where you made the first stitch, then bring it back up through on the opposite side of the shape. Don't pull too tight or the shape will distort.

Step 3

Continue making these parallel stitches, from one side of the shape to the other, until your shape is full. Fasten off the thread at the back of your work.

French Knot Perfect for flower centres, embroidered trees, or interesting patterns.

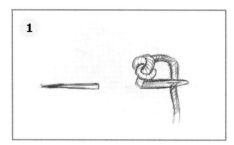

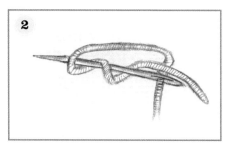

Step 1

Pull the needle through to the right side where you want the knot positioned. Wind the thread twice around the needle and insert the needle very close to where the thread came through to the right side.

Step 2

Holding the stitch with the thumb, pull the needle through to the wrong side and secure the thread, or bring it through to the right side where you want to place another knot.

Satin Stitch Use rows of close, straight stitches to fill many different shapes for interesting embroideries.

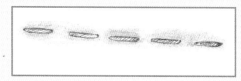

Step 1

Lay a line of running stitches along the line that you want to sew and fasten off. Now choose another colour of thread or keep the same thread, and change to a blunt-ended darning needle, depending on the size of your running stitches.

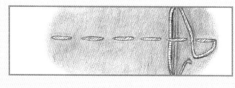

Step 2

Starting at one end of your running stitch line, bring the needle through to the right side, close to the start of the first stitch. Using the blunt end of your needle, weave the thread through your foundation line of stitches, taking care not to pull too tightly.

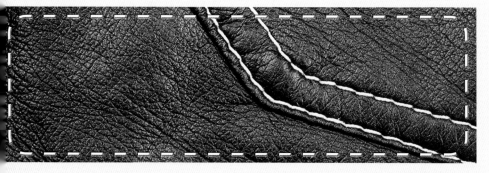

Basic Stitches

Once you have mastered the basic stitches you can add extra detail to garments with more decorative techniques.
Here are a few more stitches to increase your sewing repertoire.

Lazy Dazy Sometimes called the 'detached chain stitch', you'll most often find it used to make flowers due to the petal shape. Perfect for a quick embellishment.

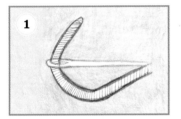  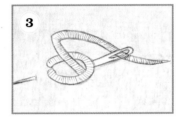 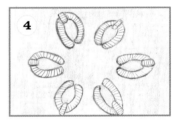

Step 1

Mark on the fabric with a fading marker where you want the stitches placed. Now bring the needle and thread through to the right side at the base of the stitch position. Take the needle down again, very close to this, but don't pull the thread through.

Step 2

Bring the tip of the needle to right side of the fabric to the length that you want your 'petal' to be, making sure the needle point goes over the thread loop and pull through.

Step 3

Take the needle back down to make a small securing stitch and adjust the loop to the shape desired.

Step 4

You can group the stitches together to make a flower formation, or add them to a stem-stitched line to give the look of leaves on a stem.

Bullion Knots Wind the thread around your needle, to create these effective, large knots.

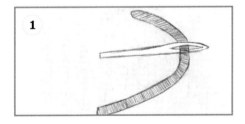 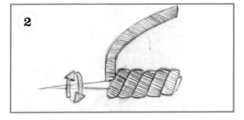 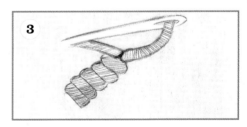

Step 1

Bring the needle up through the fabric where you want to place the stitch and take it back down the same distance that you want the knot to be, but don't pull the thread all the way through.

Step 2

Bring the needle and thread up at the first position and wind the thread from the first stitch around the point by rotating the needle around the thread.

Step 3

Hold the wound thread close to the fabric with the thumb of your other hand and gently pull the needle and thread through. Take the needle down at the other end of the stitch to secure.

Laid Trailing Stitch
Make short stitches over a thread of the same colour for a 3D feel.

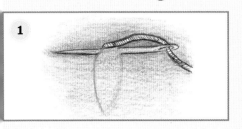

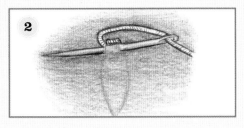

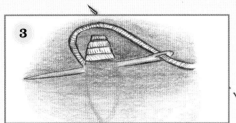

Step 1
Take your needle through to the wrong side of your fabric where you want the line to start, leaving a tail end that is the same length as the line you are creating. Place the loose thread over your work, roughly in the pattern you want to embroider.

Step 2
Bring the needle up, close to the start of the line. Now take the needle down on the other side of the tail thread and pick up a small bit of fabric beneath the loose thread (as if to encompass the thread).

Step 3
The next and all consecutive stitches should be placed close to the previous one. Continue in this manner until the length of the tail thread has been covered.

Long and Short Stitch
Use this technique to fill in large areas of your embroidery.

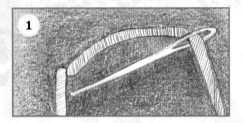

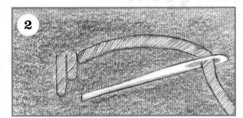

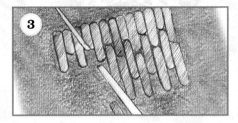

Step 1
Bring the needle up through the fabric where you want to place the stitch and take it back down the same distance that you want the knot to be, but don't pull the thread all the way through.

Step 2
Bring the needle and thread up at the first position and wind the thread from the first stitch around the point by rotating the needle around the thread.

Step 3
Hold the wound thread close to the fabric with the thumb of your other hand and gently pull the needle and thread through. Take the needle down at the other end of the stitch to secure.

Stem Stitch
By placing short stitches close to each other you can create flowing lines. Great for embroidering swirls, flower stems and other abstract shapes.

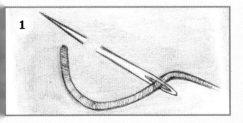

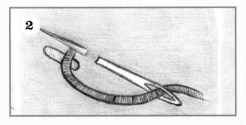

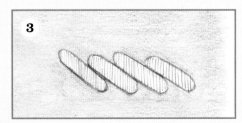

Step 1
It is best work this stitch from left to right. Bring the thread through the fabric where you want the line to start. Then push the needle through to the stitch width, and up again halfway along and to the side the first stitch length.

Step 2
Push the needle through for the next stitch width and bring it up halfway along and to the side of the previous stitch as you did in step 1.

Step 3
Continue making stitches in this way until you have filled the area needed.

SEWING
TERMS

Our quick reference guide to the sewing terminology that you'll find on the patterns.

Appliqué - Sewing a piece of fabric on top of another for decorative reasons. When done by machine, a satin stitch (tight zigzag) is often used.

Backstitching - Sewing back and forth over the same stitches to lock the end or the beginning of a line of sewing.

Batting - The filling in a quilt. It can be fiberfill, cotton, wool, or other material that is flattened and usually bought by the metre or yard. It is the middle of the quilt sandwich. Also known as wadding.

Bias - Runs diagonally to the straight grain of the fabric. Fabric cut on the bias has more stretch

Basting - The sewing of a temporary stitch. The stitches are large so as to be easily removed. They can be sewn by hand or machine but always with a view to being able to remove them easily.

Binding - Encasing the raw edges of a blanket or quilt with another piece of fabric. Binding can be bought pre-made or made yourself.

Blanket Stitch - A hand or machine stitch that is used to neaten the edge of a blanket, buttonhole or other seam line.

Casing - An envelope of sorts, usually along a waistline or a cuff, which encases elastic or drawstrings, etc.

Darn - To repair a hole by using stitches going back and forth that fill the hole. Some sewing machines come with darning attachments and stitches, which can also be used for free-motion quilting.

Embellish - To add special stitching, appliqués or other decorations to your sewing project.

Facing - Fabric sewn on the raw edge of a garment piece, which is turned under and serves as a finish for the edge as well.

Fat Quarter - A quilting term that refers to the size of a piece of fabric. A fat quarter is ¼ yard of fabric, about 18in x 22in, as opposed to a regular ¼ yard, which is 9in x 45in.

Finish (an edge) - To turn under 0.5cm (¼in) and stitch or serge the edge so that it doesn't fray or have too much bulk.

Fuse - The use of a special material that melts to 'glue' two layers together. The fusing works by being melted with an iron.

Fusible Web - Is available in a variety of weights and sizes.

Gathering - A method of easing a seam to allow insertion of sleeves and other rounded pattern pieces. To gather the seam, two parallel lines are sewn on the right side of the fabric. Long tails of thread are left for gathering. The bobbin threads (on the wrong side of the fabric) are held on either end of the seam and gently tugged, gathering the fabric evenly.

Grain - The direction of the fabric that runs parallel to the selvedge.

Hem - An edge that is turned under to the inside of a sewn item, and sewn.

Interfacing - An unseen addition to various parts of a garment, which adds body that the fabric alone would not add. Interfacing is available in many weights, in woven, knitted and non-woven forms as well as fusible and sew-in forms.

Inseam - The seam on a trouser leg that runs from the crotch to the hem.

Mitre - A technique that gives a corner a smooth, tidy finish, neatly squaring the corners while creating a diagonal seam from the point of the corner to the inside edge. Often used for the corners of a quilt binding.

Notion - A term used for any item used for sewing other than the fabric and the machine.

Pressing - A different process from ironing. Instead of running the iron across the fabric, you gently lift the iron to press a new area so as not to distort the fabric grain.

Raglan Sleeve - A type of sleeve that extends in one piece fully to the collar, leaving a diagonal seam from armpit to collarbone.

Right Side - The right side of the fabric is the side that the design is on. Sometimes a fabric has no discernible right side, so then it is up to the sewer to decide which is the right side.

Rotary Cutter - A cutting tool used in quilting to cut fabric instead of scissors. Shaped like a pizza cutter, it is perfect for cutting long strips of fabric or many layers at once.

Running Stitch - A simple stitch that is often used for basting or as the basis (marking) for another, more decorative stitch.

Serger - A type of sewing machine that stitches the seam, encases the seam with thread, and cuts off excess fabric at the same time. These are used for construction of garments with knit fabrics mostly, or to finish seams of any fabric.

Seam Allowance - The area between the stitching and raw, cut edge of the fabric. The most common seam allowances are ¼in, ½in and 5/8in. Your pattern should say which seam allowance you are to use.

Selvedge - The edges of the fabric that has the manufacturer's information. The information on a selvedge may include colour dots in the order that the colours were printed on to the fabric and lines to indicate the repeat of the pattern printed on the fabric.

Straight Stitch - The regular stitch that most sewing machines make.

Top Stitch - A sometimes decorative, sometimes functional stitch that is usually ¼in from the edge of a seam.

Tension - There are two types of tension on your sewing machine - the thread and bobbin tensions.

Tack - To sew a few stitches in one spot, by hand or by machine sewing, to secure one item to another.

Wrong Side - The side of the fabric that has no design on it or that you don't want facing outwards. Sometimes there is no discernible wrong side to a fabric.

Zigzag Stitch - A stitch that goes one way and then the other and provides a nice finish to a seam to prevent fraying, it can also be used as a decorative stitch.

Clothes

Dive into a variety of exciting projects in this fabulous clothing section and create your very own vibrant, one-of-a-kind garments that you'll love to wear time and time again.

Jersey Dress

Make this simple yet gorgeous jersey dress from one piece of fabric – no cutting is required, just sewing with elastic for an easy-fitting style.

About this Pattern

3 ●●●○○ **Difficult**

MATERIALS

Double-width jersey – 1m x 1.25m (39in x 49in)

Elastic, 0.5-1cm (¼–½in) wide (see table and pattern notes for details)

Shirring elastic – 1–2 reels

Spare bobbin (for winding elastic)

PATTERN NOTES

We've given suggested elastic requirements in the finished size table, but alternatively, you could measure your chest (above the bust) and take 10cm from the measurements. Pull the elastic around you before you cut – it should not be loose (otherwise the dress will fall down!) but equally, it should not be so tight as to dig into your skin.

It takes a surprising amount of shirring elastic to complete this project, so make sure you have enough. White shirring elastic will be fine for most projects. Choose a matching colour if your fabric is semi-transparent, or choose a contrasting colour and stitch the elastic on the right side of the fabric.

We recommend using a quilter's guide bar when spacing the elastic – it's not essential but will save you a great deal of measuring time!

All seam allowances are 0.5cm, unless otherwise stated.

Step
FORM A TUNNEL FOR THE ELASTIC

Distinguish the width of the fabric from the length – the width will be a larger measurement than the length. The length will be 1m (1yd). Along the width, fold the fabric over by 0.5cm (¼in), then fold over again by 1.5cm (⅝in), in the same way as a hem would be made. Stitch this down so that it forms a 1cm (½in) tunnel. Do not add the elastic yet.

Step 2
FIRST SHIRRING LINE

Wind the shirring elastic onto the bobbin, stretching it slightly as you go. Do not overfill the bobbin. Your top thread should match or contrast with your fabric, as it will be visible on the right side of the dress. Set your stitch length (on straight stitch) to at least 4. Test on a scrap of the fabric.

"Made from a single rectangle of jersey fabric, this dress couldn't be easier to put together!"

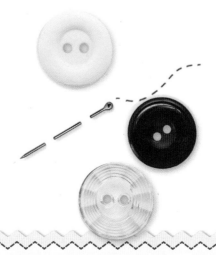

The fabric will be sewn on the right side. Attach the quilter's guide bar so that it is 2cm (¾in) away from where you will be stitching. Use the stitching of the tunnel as a guide to keeping your next stitch line straight. You will stitch a straight line underneath the line of the elastic tunnel you made previously. Starting from one end (without back-stitching to secure), sew along the length of the fabric.

At the end, do not secure the stitching with back-stitches. Start and finish less than 0.5cm (¼in) away from the edges. Note: If you do not have a quilter's guide-bar, mark out the rows with tailor's chalk at an equal distance apart. Follow them with the stitches.

Step 3
NEXT SHIRRING LINE

Once again, line up the quilter's guide bar with the line you just stitched 2cm (¾in) away. As you sew the second line, make sure you pull the previous line of stitching so that the fabric is flat. This will help you to keep the lines straight and keep the gathers even.

If the bobbin elastic runs out mid-row, simply refill the bobbin, then stitch over the last few stitches sewn. These can be tidied up when you tie off the other ends.

Continue in this way until you have made a section that will sufficiently cover the bust area – measure against yourself to gauge when it's done.

Step 4
NEATEN ENDS

Tie off all the ends individually, then stitch over them in a long line of straight stitch, 0.5cm (¼in) from the edge, on both sides. You will stitch over them again when sewing the side seam.

Step 5
INSERT THICK ELASTIC

Cut your elastic to length. Thread it through the tunnel across the top of the dress – pin one end to the fabric so that you don't lose it within the tunnel. Spread the gathers across the full width of the dress. Secure the elastic ends together with a few stitches, then tuck the join in the elastic into one side.

Note: For larger dress sizes, the elastic will be looser than the shirring, but this will be fine because the shirring will stretch as necessary.

Step 6
STITCH THE BACK SEAM

Fold your fabric in half along the length of the dress, with right sides together. Pin the back seams together. Select a stretch stitch on your machine and sew using a 1cm (½in) seam allowance. Jersey doesn't tend to fray so there is no need to finish the seam, but if you wish, you could finish the seam with a zig-zag stitch.

Step 7
HEM

Since jersey doesn't fray, your fabric may not need to be hemmed. If you do wish to hem the bottom of the dress, fold under by 1cm (½in) and press, then fold under by a further 1cm (½in) (to enclose the raw edge) and stitch with a stretch stitch.

Step 8
STRAPS

Straps can be added, if necessary. These could be pre-made bra straps, decorative elastic or fabric-covered elastic.

FINISHED SIZE TABLE

DRESS SIZE	8	10	12	14	16	18	20	UK
BUST	77	82	87	92	97	102	107	cm
WAIST	59	64	69	74	79	84	89	cm
HIP	83	88	93	98	103	108	113	cm
ELASTIC REQUIRED	67	72	77	82	87	92	97	cm

Delilah Skirt

A simple A-line skirt pattern that is fun to make and to wear.

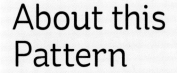

About this Pattern

2 ○●○○○ Intermediate

SIZE
UK dress sizes 10, 12, 14, 16

MATERIALS
1.8m (2yd) upholstery fabric
15cm (6in) zip
3.5m (4yd) of 2.5cm (1in) wide
velvet ribbon

TEMPLATES
Please see step 1.

Step 1
CREATE PATTERN

Measure your waist and add on 4cm (1½in). Divide this number by 2. Your skirt pattern needs to be this amount wide at the top and twice as wide at the bottom. Make the length as long as you want the skirt to be, making sure you allow for the hem and skirt casing. Cut front and back panels using this template.

Step 2
FINISH EDGES

Zigzag stitch all the raw edges of the pattern pieces to ensure they are neat.

Step 3
INSERT ZIP AND JOIN SEAMS

With right-sides facing, pin down one side seam. Mark 15cm (6in) from the waistband and sew to the hem leaving a 1cm (½in) allowance. Press the seam to the waistband. Pin in place the zip, right-side to the wrong-side, and attach using the zip foot on your sewing machine. Sew the second seam the same way.

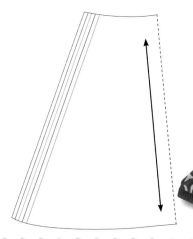

Step 4
TURN WAISTBAND

Turn the waistband over 0.5cm (¼in), press with an iron and stitch in place. Attach the velvet ribbon to the outside waistband, ensuring that the edges are neat where they meet the zip.

Step 5
BOTTOM HEM

Attach the velvet ribbon to the bottom hem of the skirt, using a matching thread and ensuring that it is level all the way around.

Layered Skirt

A simple A-line skirt pattern that is fun to make and to wear.

About this Pattern

3 ⚫⚫⚫◯◯ **Difficult**

Step 1
CUT TOP LAYER

Refer to the table below and cut a piece of fabric measuring, 109 (114, 119, 124, 129, 134) cm, 42 (44, 46, 48, 50, 52) in long, by 30cm (12in) wide.

Step 2
PREPARE TOP LAYER

Turn the top of the fabric over by 0.5cm (¼in) and press. Turn over again towards the inside 2.5cm (1in) and sew in place, leaving a channel so that you can thread elastic through for the waistband. Zigzag stitch the bottom edge of the rectangle and then sew the ends of the fabric together to form a tube.

Step 3
MIDDLE LAYER

Cut a piece of fabric measuring, 142 (149, 155, 162, 168, 175) cm, 55 (59, 61, 63, 66, 68) in long, by 35cm (14in) wide. Again, zigzag stitch the bottom of the rectangle and also the top before sewing the ends together like a tube. To make the simple gathers, sew a zigzag stitch along the edge to be gathered. Thread an embroidery needle with thick thread. Using the needle thread the yarn under the stitches. Pull the yarn, gathering the fabric to desired width. Secure well at the end to keep the gathers from coming out. Distribute the gathers evenly and then stitch across the gathers with a 5mm seam to keep them in place. Remove the thick thread if you desire.

MATERIALS

Use a lightweight cord fabric. See below for amounts needed and follow instructions in the text for cutting.

2cm (¾in) wide elastic for waistband.

Size (UK)	8	10	12	14	16	18	20	
Actual hip measurement	90	94	99	104	109	114	120	cm
	35	37	38	40	42	44	47	in
Material needed	2	2	2	2.5	2.5	2.5	3	metres
	2½	2½	2½	3	3	3	3½	yards

Step 4
ATTACH MIDDLE LAYER

To attach to the bottom of your first tube, keep the top tier of your skirt, right-side facing out.

Step 5
HEM

Cut a piece of fabric measuring 184 (193, 201, 210, 218, 226) cm, 72½ (76, 80, 83, 86, 89) in long, by 30cm (12in) wide. Again, repeat the zig zag stitch, sewing the ends together like a tube and gathering stitches as in step 3. Attach to the bottom of your second panel using the same method in step 4. Sew a 2.5cm (1in) hem at the bottom of this final third panel.

Step 6
WAISTBAND

Thread elastic through the channel you made at the top of the skirt. Adjust it to fit comfortably, cut the elastic and sew the gap closed.

T-Shirt to
Tie-front Wrap

This restyle is a perfect, simple way to update last year's cropped, oversized t-shirt and jazz it up for this summer.

About this Pattern

1 ●○○○○ Beginner

MATERIALS

Oversized cropped T-shirt
Bias binding - 1m (1yd)
Selection of quirky buttons

Step 1
MARK UP T-SHIRT

Mark the centre point of the front of the T-shirt and draw a straight line from the top to the bottom with a fabric pencil. Cut the T-shirt along this line.

Step 2
ATTACH BINDING

Sew the bias binding to the cut edges, starting from the top. Open out the binding, and pin so that the edge of the binding and top are even. Stitch along the binding fold crease then fold the binding to the wrong-side of the top, encasing the raw edges and hand stitch the underside in place. Alternatively, sandwich the cut edge within the folded binding and pin. Select a wide decorative stitch on the sewing machine and thread to match the binding. Sew over the edges, attaching binding at the front and underside as you go. Leave a length of bias binding hanging at the bottom of the T-shirt for ties.

Step 3
SEW BUTTONS

Sew the buttons on one side of the T-shirt at the top near the bias binding. Then repeat with the other side. The buttons may add a lot of weight to the top of the T-shirt so join the cut gap again by sewing a suitable button of your choice over the top of the overlapped fabric and your refashion is complete!

"This is the perfect way to use up any spare fabric scraps and buttons."

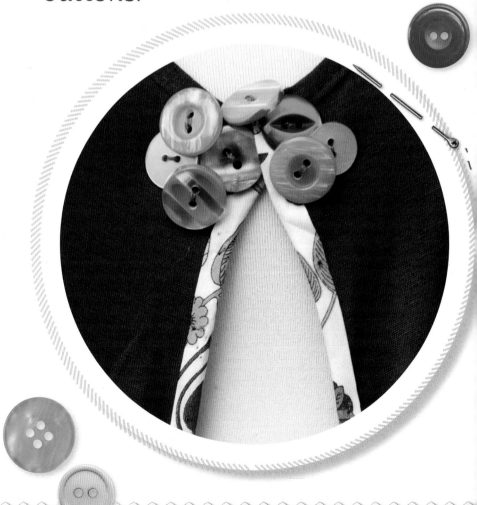

Top Tip

Add a square of fusible interfacing underneath the button area to give more support to the garment top.

Headscarf Top

This restyle is a perfect, simple way to update last year's cropped, oversized t-shirt and jazz it up for this summer.

About this Pattern

1 ●○○○○ **Beginner**

FINISHED SIZE

This top will fit a UK size 6–12. If you need a larger size you can follow these simple instructions by using larger scarves, or squares of fabric with neatened edges.

MATERIALS

2 silky headscarves, measuring approx. 50cm (20in) square

Handsewing needle

Matching cotton thread

PATTERN NOTES

Enjoy choosing the headscarves for this project. Matching ones would be nice, as would complete contrasts.

Step 1
CUT FABRIC

Cut two out of the 3 fat quarters as per the cutting list.

Step 2
JOIN FAT QUARTERS

Sew the fat quarters together using ¼in seam allowance, using the photograph below as a guide.

Step 3
JOIN EDGES

With right-sides facing, fold the rectangle in half widthways, sew for approx. 15in in from either end or to within 3in of your shoulder.

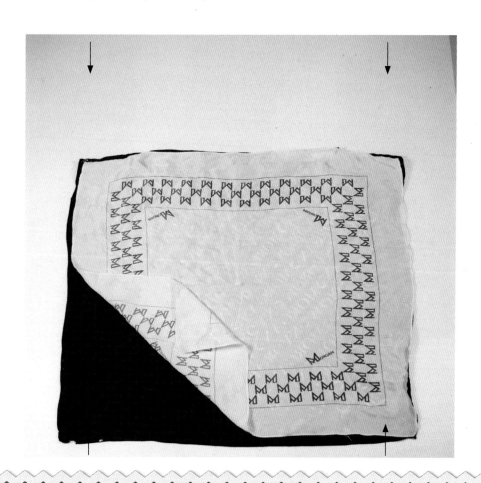

"Use 2 different scarves for a reversible top or the same ones for something simple."

Drawstring Skirt

Make your little one as pretty as a picture in this simple-to-make skirt!

About this Pattern

1 ●○○○○ Beginner

Step 1
CUT FABRIC

Cut a piece of fabric as per the cutting list.

Step 2
HEM AND CREATE CHANNEL FOR ELASTIC

With the wrong-side facing up, turn a 2cm (¾in) hem at the bottom of the fabric and sew into place. Turn the top of the fabric down 1cm (⅜in), press and then turn down a further 3cm (1⅛in) to create a channel for the elastic to be inserted. Press and then sew into place.

Step 3
TRIM BOTTOM EDGE

If you wish, this is the time to sew on your decorative trim at the bottom of the skirt. With the right-side facing up, pin your ribbon, ricrac or chosen embellishment to the bottom of your skirt and sew into place.

Step 4
SEW SIDE SEAMS

Zig-zag stitch the raw edges of the skirt; then, with right-sides facing, sew side seams, ensuring that you sew through only one layer of the fabric at the top where the elastic channel is.

Step 5
INSERT ELASTIC

Insert your elastic through the waistband channel and secure. Sew the gap closed and the skirt is ready to wear!

Top Tip

You can use any fabric for this skirt – dressmaking or quilting weight cotton works best, but upholstery weight will still work, albeit resulting in a heavier weight skirt.

MATERIALS

1m (1 yd) of fabric
1m (1 yd) of elastic for waistband
1–2m (1–2 yd) of contrast ribbon, ricrac or other embellishment for bottom of skirt (optional)

FINISHED SIZE

2–3 years – 30cm (12in) long
4–5 years – 35cm (14in) long
6–7 years – 40cm (16in) long
8–9 years – 45cm (18in) long
10–11 years – 50cm (20in) long

CUTTING LIST

Age – width x length
2–3 years – 1m (1 yd) x 38cm (15in)
4–5 years – 1m (1 yd) x 43cm (17in)
6–7 years – 1m (1 yd) x 48cm (19in)
8–9 years – 1m (1 yd) x 53cm (21in)
10–11 years – 1m (1 yd) x 58cm (23in)

Pillowcase
Dresses

These dresses were made from odd pillowcases.
They're great to use as painting overalls.

About this Pattern

1 ⬤◯◯◯◯ Beginner

Step 1
PREPARATION

Wash and iron your pillowcase.

Step 2
CUT FOR LENGTH

Measure the distance from the child's shoulder blade to where you want the dress to fall to and add 2.5cm (1in).

Mark this on the pillowcase and cut off the closed edge at the point you have marked.

Step 3
MAKE ARMHOLES

Fold the pillowcase in half widthwise and mark out the armholes as shown in the sketch below. The piece you cut out should be 5cm wide and 15cm deep. Cut out the arm holes.

SIZE
One pillowcase will make a dress to fit a child up to the age of 10.

MATERIALS
- 1 pillow case
- Approx 1m (1 yd) of ribbon

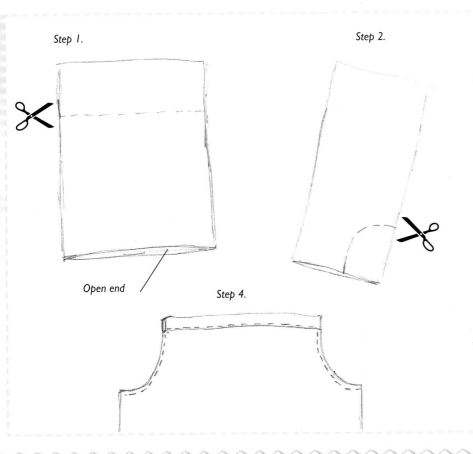

Step 1.

Open end

Step 2.

Step 4.

White version made from flannel pillowcase and embellished with buttons. Pink version made from flannel pillowcase and armholes bound with the same fabric that was used for the ribbon tie.

The bright patterned version made from a handmade pillowcase bought from a flea market.

Step 4

SEAM ARMHOLES

Turn inside out and press a 1.5cm (½in) seam around the armholes to the wrong side. Stitch into place.

Step 5

CHANNEL FOR RIBBON

Fold over 2.5cm (1in) at the top of the front of the pillowcase to form a casing for the ribbon to go through. Stitch into place. Repeat for the back.

Step 6

ADD TIES

Cut the ribbon in half. Thread one piece through the front and one piece through the back channel. Pull and gather, then tie at the top of the shoulders to keep the

Step 5.

dress on. Alternatively, if you prefer, move the ribbons through the channel so that the tied sections are not showing.

Step 7

EMBELLISH

The hem at the bottom of the pillowcase makes the hem at the bottom of your dress. If you prefer, you can hem along the 'envelope' part of the case and cut out the excess fabric. Decorate with, ribbon or other finishing as desired.

Embellishment by
Appliqué

Give a T-shirt new life with appliqué stitching.

About this Pattern

1 ●○○○○ Beginner

Step 1
FIND APPLIQUÉ DESIGN

Draw or copy a design suitable for appliqué. Children's colouring books are a good source as the illustrations have simple outlines or create a flower with circles, ovals and leaf shapes. Divide the design into parts of different colours.

Step 2
IRON FUSIBLE WEBBING

Cut rectangles of fusible webbing large enough for each part of the design and iron these to the wrong side of the coloured fabrics. On the paper, draw the outline of each shape. If the design is not symmetrical remember to draw the shape in reverse so that it will appear the correct way when stuck down.

Step 3
CUT SHAPES

Cut out each part of the shape and peel off the backing paper. Arrange these in position, a little like a jigsaw, then iron carefully to fuse them in place (fig 1).

Sew in place with either a contrast thread or one that matches depending on the effect required (contrasting thread will form a bold outline and make the design more prominent). Use a zigzag stitch with a reduced length to produce a satin stitch that gives a bolder line. The approximate setting of the stitch will be 3mm wide and 0.3mm long. This may be marked in stitches per inch on other machines in which case the setting should be approximately eight stitches per inch wide and 20 stitches per inch long. Try the stitch on an off-cut

FINISHED SIZE

This will vary according to your design and the item you are embellishing.

MATERIALS

Plain T-shirt

Brightly coloured plain or printed fabric scraps to use for the appliqué designs

One pack of fusible webbing Contrasting or matching sewing thread as desired

Tear-away stabiliser

of fabric and adjust to achieve a solid band of stitching before starting to sew on the design.

Step 4
ADD STITCHING

Complete the design with any other lines and stitches over the appliqué or round the collar, cuffs or hem of the T-shirt. Many modern sewing machines have a wide range of decorative stitches to choose from but a range of simple straight and zigzag stitches can look just as effective, too.

Fig 1.

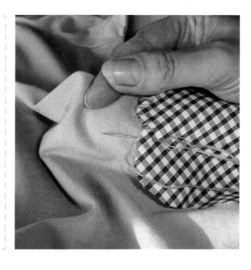

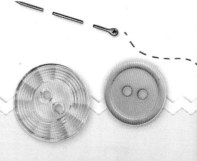

Top Tip

When sewing directly onto the T-shirt fabric use a tear away stabiliser underneath the stabiliser tears away completely afterwards.

No sewing machine?

If you do not have a sewing machine it is easy to sew the appliqué in place with blanket stitches sewn by hand. Use an embroidery thread (either three strands of stranded embroidery thread or pearle cotton) in a contrasting colour and form the stitches around the outside of the design.

The addition of a simple appliqué motif can make an unloved T-shirt into a uniquely designed creation. Recycling or up-cycling clothing has been a popular theme in recent years. It allows a 'new' garment to be created with little or no cost to you or to the environment.

Applique know-how

● Appliqué is a technique where, as the name implies, a piece of fabric is applied to the surface of another. The method produces a bold embellishment that is easy to create compared with the more time-consuming skill of embroidery. It has the added benefit of being 'green' as it can use up unwanted fabrics; off-cuts from other projects or unwanted, out-dated or worn-out clothing. All are perfect for producing appliqué designs.

● Bondaweb is a heat-fusible glue layer on a paper base. The glue is in the form of a film backed with the paper (to make handling easier), which melts and fuses when heated. Iron it to the back of a fabric, cut out a shape, peel off the backing paper and place it where required on a garment then iron it in position. This does away with the need to tack or baste the shape in place by hand before sewing it securely in position.

● Stabiliser is a bonded layer of material used under the fabric during stitching to support the stitches and allow a better finish to be produced. The most common variety is the tearaway stabiliser that is torn off after stitching. Other varieties of this include soluble (washaway) and heataway stabilisers.

● Satin stitch is a machine zigzag stitch which has been shortened to give a bold line.

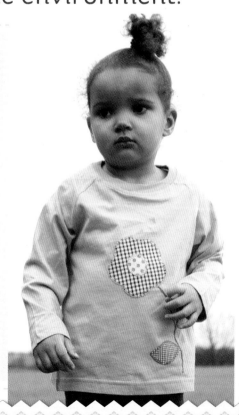

Top Tip

An artfully placed appliqué can be used to cover up a stubborn stain!

Simple Children's
Clothes

Sometimes the very best revamps
are the most simple.

About this Pattern

1 ●○○○○ Beginner

Lay the T-shirt down on a flat surface and measure all around the bottom, recording the measurement on a piece of paper.

The fabric for the skirt needs to measure approximately 25cm (10in) deep by two times the circumference of your T-shirt. Cut to size.

Fold the bottom of the fabric up 1cm (³/₈in) and press. Fold up again and hand stitch hem in place. Press the side seams in by 1cm (³/₈in) and then repeat. With right-sides facing, stitch the side seam together.

Sew two rows of large stitches around the top of the skirt to use as gathering stitches. Do not secure the end.

With the T-shirt the correct way up on the table, place the skirt piece inside out and around the T-shirt so that the neat hem is at the top and the gathered edge is at the bottom of the T-shirt.

The T-shirt should fit neatly inside the skirt. Pull the gathering strings until the skirt is the same size as the T-shirt.

Pin and then sew in place with the gathered edge of the skirt fitting inside the T-shirt.

MATERIALS

A T-shirt that fits your child
0.5m (½ yd) of lightweight fabric (voile or quilters cotton works well)
Matching thread
Needle

TIME TAKEN

An hour